Dinosaurs

Created by Gallimard Jeunesse,
Claude Delafosse, and Jame's Prunier
Illustrated by Jame's Prunier and Henri Galeron

A FIRST DISCOVERY BOOK

SCHOLASTIC INC. Cartwheel B·O·O·K·S ®

New York   Toronto   London   Auckland   Sydney
Mexico City   New Delhi   Hong Kong   Buenos Aires

Dinosaurs lived long ago in prehistoric times.
Baby dinosaurs hatched from eggs.

Protoceratops babies

Tuatara

Crocodile

Many reptiles
are descendants of dinosaurs.

Not all dinosaurs were alike.
Some were as small as turkeys,
while others were as big as...

Compsognathus

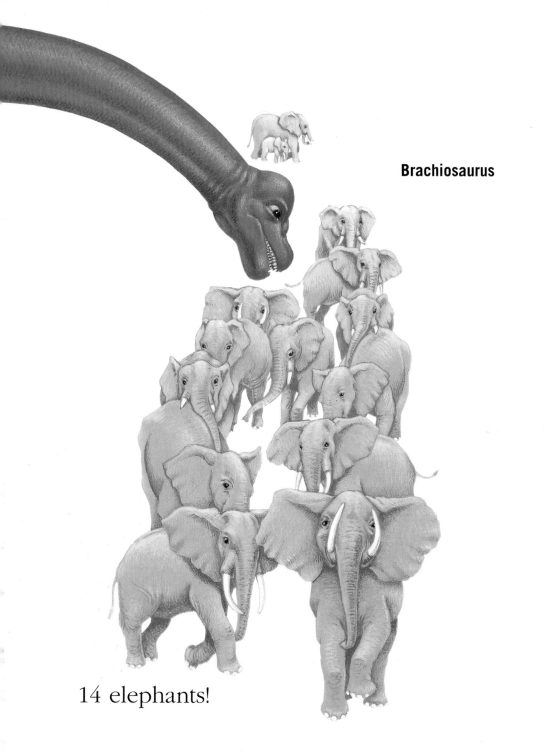

Brachiosaurus

14 elephants!

Protoceratops

Some dinosaurs, like these, were herbivores.
They only ate plants.
Others were carnivores.
They ate meat.

Triceratops

The legs of some dinosaurs were as
wide as tree trunks.

Dinosaurs roamed the Earth for nearly
150 million years until they died off
and became extinct. Many years later,
people found dinosaur bones and footprints.
These are called fossils.

**Some fossils are bones that
have turned to stone.**

Scientists called paleontologists study dinosaur bones.

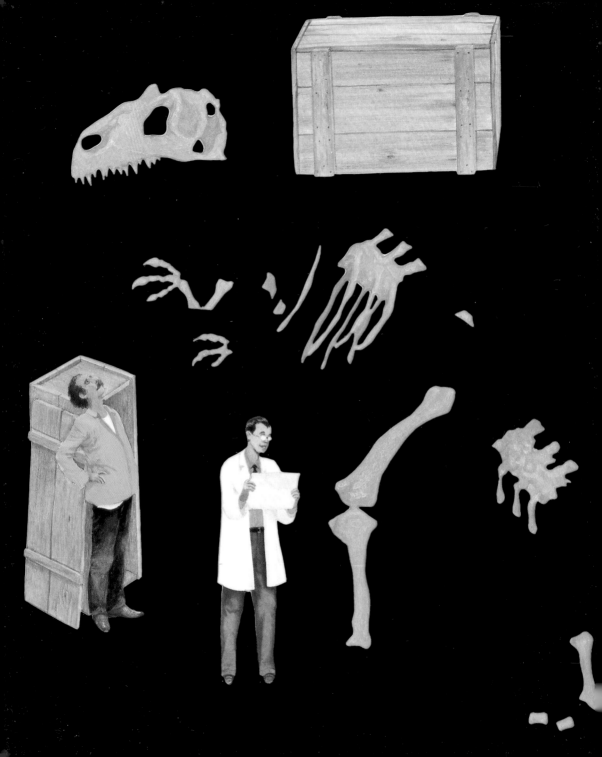

They bring the bones
to museums, where
they put them back
together to make
dinosaur skeletons.

Iguanodon

The Iguanodon usually walked on two legs, but sometimes it used all four. Iguanodon was a plant eater. It probably used its spiky thumb to defend itself against enemies, who were meat eaters.

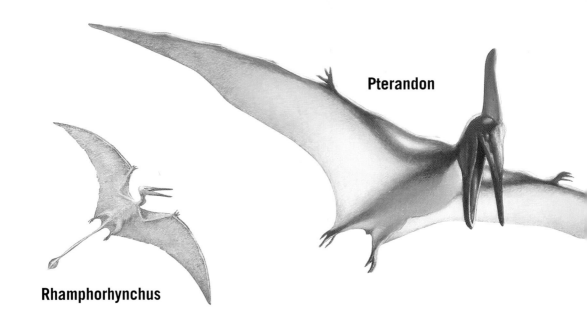

Pterandon

Rhamphorhynchus

These flying
reptiles lived
at the same
time as the
dinosaurs.

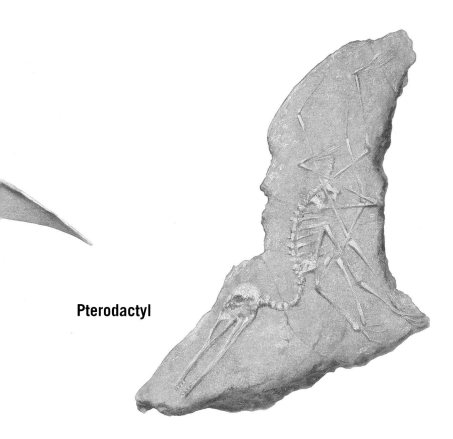

Pterodactyl

Besides fossils
of reptiles,
other fossils
are leaf prints
left in mud
that turned
to stone.

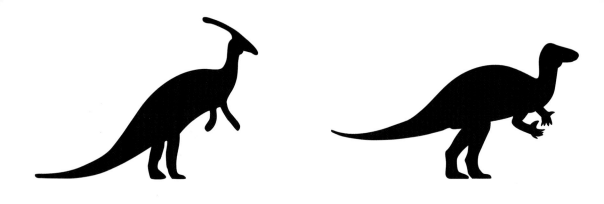

Some dinosaur tails were short. Others were very long. Paleontologists discover the length of tails when they put together tailbone fossils.

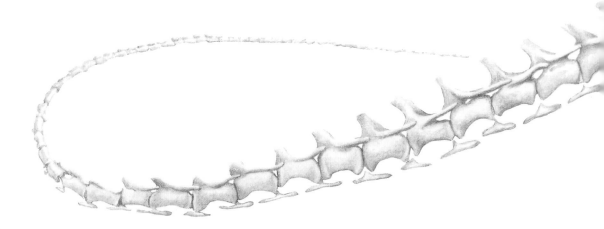

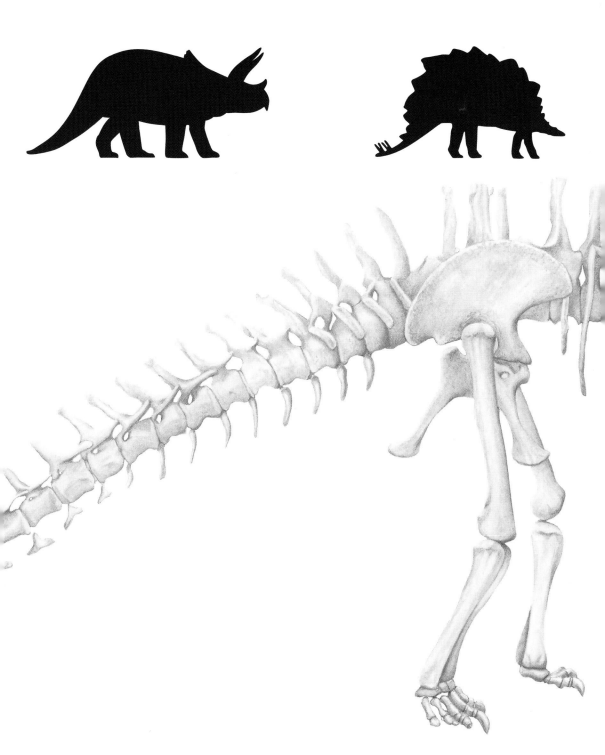

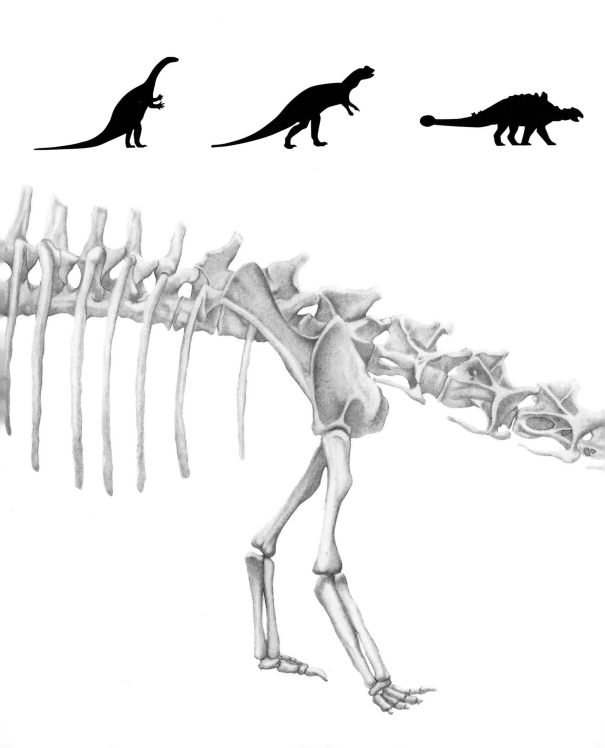

Dinosaur necks came in different lengths, too. Diplodocus had such a long neck that it could eat leaves from the tops of trees.

Diplodocus skeleton

One of the longest dinosaurs, Diplodocus was about 80 feet from nose to tail. That's as long as two buses in a row!

Mammoths were huge animals
that lived after the dinosaurs.
Ancestors of the elephant,
mammoths are now extinct.

On TV, people fight dinosaurs,
but that's all make-believe.
Dinosaurs lived on Earth
long before people did.

There are many toy
models of dinosaurs.
Like toy model cars,
toy dinosaurs are a
popular collector's item.

Films show that the earliest
prehistoric people hunted
mammoths for food!

Learn the different dinosaur names by matching each dinosaur shadow to its picture on the right.

Triceratops

Edmontosaurus

Ankylosaurus

Stegosaurus

Iguanodon

Tyrannosaurus Rex

Compsognathus

Brachiosaurus

Diplodocus

Why did the dinosaur
become extinct?
No one knows for sure.